T0122223

The Raven's LUNCH

PATRICIA TORSEN

I dedicate this book to my daughter Michele White who without her assistance this book and the previous book would not have been published. Through her timeless dedication, to helping her mother these children's books are being shared with the public.

Archway Publishing books may be ordered through booksellers or by contacting:

Archway Publishing
1663 Liberty Drive
Bloomington, IN 47403
www.archwaypublishing.com
844-669-3957

Because of the dynamic nature of the Internet, any web addresses or links contained in this book may have changed since publication and may no longer be valid. The views expressed in this work are solely those of the author and do not necessarily reflect the views of the publisher, and the publisher hereby disclaims any responsibility for them.

Any people depicted in stock imagery provided by Getty Images are models, and such images are being used for illustrative purposes only.
Certain stock imagery © Getty Images.

ISBN: 978-1-6657-0202-7 (sc)
ISBN: 978-1-6657-0201-0 (hc)
ISBN: 978-1-6657-0203-4 (e)

Print information available on the last page.

Archway Publishing rev. date: 6/28/2021

ARCHWAY
PUBLISHING

One day while Patty was riding back and forth on the crane track, she got hungry. She realized she hadn't taken a break. She decided she would stop stacking lumber, and go get a snack.

She went into her lunch bag and took out a bag of popcorn to pop, and went to the lunch room and popped it. She took the popcorn back out to where she was working at the sawmill, and started eating some. She realized she had dropped a couple of pieces, but decided some little animals would be picking them up, so she left them.

Soon she was riding back and forth on the crane, stacking lumber in piles again. Then, out of the corner of her eye she saw something moving.... "What was that?" Something moved Again....Then Patty saw what it was!

Cecil Raven had come to pick up the popcorn. He seemed to be really enjoying it. She wondered if he might like some more. She threw some more popcorn in his direction. He grabbed a piece in his mouth and flew off.

A few minutes later Cecil Raven came back, picked up another piece of popcorn, then flew off. She threw several pieces of popcorn for him. That was fun. Patty went back to work, stacking lumber with the crane. Cecil Raven had enough popcorn for today.

The next day Landon and Wesley were out in the parking lot for their lunch break. They were visiting and eating their lunches. Landon saw Cecil Raven and threw him a piece of his sandwich. Cecil Raven came, picked up the piece of sandwich and flew off.

Then he came back, and Landon threw him another piece of his sandwich. Cecil Raven was very pleased, he took the piece of sandwich and flew off. He came back several times and ate pieces of sandwich and then he flew off.

Patty noticed after lunch Cecil Raven came back. He just watched and waited and then he flew off again. Days past and Cecil Raven came to get food and then he would fly off with it. Everyone thought Cecil Raven was such a nice bird, they enjoyed sharing their lunches and snacks with him.

One day when Cecil Raven came, he was not alone....Cecil Raven brought along Hannah Raven, his wife. She was a very pretty raven, as ravens go.

Cecil Raven taught her where to wait for the food and they both would pick up pieces of snacks and foods and go off to their nest. Back and forth, day after day, Patty, Landon, and Wesley fed Mr. and Mrs. Raven. Patty noticed there was a great big Fir Tree in the distance, and at times, she could see Cecil or Hannah Raven on a branch in that tree.

That must be their home she thought. It was close to the sawmill and very high so they could see along way off. One day Cecil Raven saw something by Patty's crane. He came over closer to see. Well what was that? Patty had crackers that day, and she thought Cecil Raven might like one.

Cecil Raven put his beak on the pavement and slid that cracker right in his mouth, and then he flew off.

Then Hannah Raven came by, so Patty threw a cracker out for her. Then she flew off to her nest.

15

Cecil Raven came back and Patty threw another cracker and he picked it up. Then Hannah came, Patty threw her a cracker and they both flew off to their nest.

Cecil Raven came back and Patty decided to throw 2 crackers at once so Hannah would have one also, But! Cecil Raven slid one cracker into his mouth, picked it up and put it on top of the other cracker, picked them both up and flew off.

Hannah Raven didn't get any cracker. Patty saw this and threw another cracker for Hannah Raven she picked it up and flew off to their nest.

Cecil Raven came back again, and Patty thought, "I'll throw 3 crackers this time!" "then Hannah Raven will have one too." But Cecil Raven picked up one cracker in his beak stacked it on top of another cracker, slid his beak under the two crackers, picked them up, and stacked them onto the next cracker, slid his beak under all three crackers, picked them up and flew off.

At last she thought, "I am going to put out 4 crackers," surely Hannah will get one of those. But Cecil Raven picked up 1 cracker slid it in his mouth, set it on another, picked them up and set them on another, picked them up and set them on the last one.....and flew off with them.

Hannah Raven then came back and Patty threw another cracker to her. She didn't give Cecil Raven any more crackers that day. He was being silly. He was having lots of fun with those crackers and Patty knew he wasn't eating them all.

What was he doing with all those crackers? Mr. and Mrs. Raven came back and forth for lunch snacks and other sorts of things they found good to eat. Weeks past and each day they came to get whatever was thrown to them. Landon and Wesley were giving them a great selection, and Patty threw little bits of snacks for them also. Back and forth they went with their food bits.

One day Patty, Landon and Wesley had a surprise. Cecil and Hannah Raven brought their son Jr. Raven. They were teaching him how to get food.

They taught him to be patient and what times to come and get food, and how to pick it up. Patty, Landon and Wesley gave them extra food since now there was three of their family.

The Raven Family came many times to get food and they were met with many kinds of snacks and bits of foods. It was a wonderful way to spend an afternoon and Patty, Landon, and Wesley were very good to the Raven Family. One day the sawmill closed and the Raven Family could come no more to get food and snacks.

They would not have snacks and bits from Patty, Landon and Wesley, so they flew around, looking for what they could find. They found little bits of things but it wasn't the same. They missed their friends at the sawmill, and the bits and snacks that were given to them. They missed the sawmill with all the surprises they had there.

As Cecil Raven was flying around one day he looked down by a big Fir Tree. In the yard by the tree stood someone he thought he recognized.... It was Patty! She was throwing bird seed to little birds, so Cecil Raven flew down to her. She recognized him right away. She threw him some bread and he flew off.

Soon he returned with his family. Cecil, Hannah and Raven Jr., they all chirped and chattered, they were very glad to see Patty, and she was glad to see them.

The Raven Family came back often, along with other birds. Patty fed Wrens, Robins, Blue Jays and even Pheasants came.

She was good to all the birds, and they in turn sang and chirped, and peeped to her and made her happy. And the Raven Family felt they were at home again with their friend Patty.

About the Author

Patricia Torsen is a seventy-three-year-old great-grandmother who loves to encourage young readers through her stories inspired by the animal activity she witnessed while working in a sawmill for twenty-seven years. This is the second book in a series.

Printed in the United States
by Baker & Taylor Publisher Services